THE WOLF YEARLING

POEMS

THE WOLF YEARLING

POEMS

Jeffrey C. Alfier

SILVER BIRCH PRESS
LOS ANGELES, CALIFORNIA

ISBN-13: 978-0615806440

ISBN-10: 0615806449

First Silver Birch Press Edition: May 2013

Book and cover design: Silver Birch Press

Cover photo: Justasc, Used by Permission

Contact: silverbirchpress@yahoo.com

Web: silverbirchpress.com

Mailing Address:
Silver Birch Press
P.O. Box 29458
Los Angeles, CA 90029

A little damage and a little grace…
ELIZA GILKYSON, **THINK ABOUT YOU**

ACKNOWLEDGEMENTS

Grateful acknowledgment is made to the following journals, in which these poems originally appeared, sometimes in slightly different form:

Artifact Literary Journal—"Nineveh, Texas"
Blue Collar Review—"Foreclosure in Late Autumn," "The Seasonal Worker," "Vaqueros por La Vida"
Blue Earth Review— "The Stableman"
Borderlands: Texas Poetry Review—"My Great Aunt Speaks of Nights in Hardin County"
Caesura— "A Raven Returns to the Salton Sea"
Concho River Review—"The Farmer's Daughter in Late Summer," "Last Light at Stronghold Canyon," "Land Survey in the Amargosa Valley"
Connecticut Review—"Renaming the Earth"
Crab Orchard Review— "Blues Despite the Odds"
Flint Hills Review— "First Snow in the Santa Catalinas"
Front Range Review— "My Sister Waits with Mamagrande Outside Santa Teresita's"
Georgetown Review— "Letter from Yuma to My Father Back East"
Hot Air Quarterly— "Desert Mountain Sunday"
Iodine Poetry Journal— "White Canyon"
Iron Horse Literary Review— "The Desert Elk"
James Dickey Review—"Diverting South from Buckhorn Tank"
Mangrove Review— "The Father Returning"
Mountain Gazette— "Dead Reckoning in the Puerto Blanco Mountains"
Muscle & Blood— "No Texas Beyond Our Memory"
Northridge Review— "Overheard Between Waco and Jubilee Springs"
Owen Wister Review—"Why You Can Never Cure a Small-Town Heart"
Penumbra— "Last Words to an Old Miner Leaving Albuquerque" "Nightfall on the Bajada"
Permafrost— "Winter Foothills"
Pilgrimage—"Bonnie Claire Flat, Death Valley"
Pinyon— "Near Cananea"
Raleigh Review—"Terlingua"
RE:AL— "One Son South to Rio Bravo"
Red River Review— "Homeward from Austin"
River Oak Review— "The Cotton West of Hockley County"

Ruminate—"Mapping the Migrant's Shrine"
Sage Trail—"Marquise Drive in Winter"
Santa Clara Review— "Leaving Cipriano Pass"
Sierra Nevada College Review—"The Desert Rancher on Sunday"
South Carolina Review—"Overtaking the Union Pacific"
Southwestern American Literature—"The Third Mesa"
Streetlight—"North of San Lázaro," "The Evangelist at the Brazos River"
Texas Review— "Last Words to My Daughter Transporting a Foal"
Three Coyotes— "Climbing Cap Rock Trail with My Daughter" "How We Woke One Year in Lobo, Texas"
The Saint Ann's Review— "Cowboys," "Passage Through the Cordillera"
Watershed— "Late Light in the Santa Cruz Valley"

Eliza Gilkyson. (2005). "A little damage and a little grace," excerpted from the song, "Think About You." On *Paradise Hotel* [CD]. St. Paul, MN: Red House Records. Used by permission of the artist.

The author is grateful to Bloodaxe Books of Northumberland, UK, for permission to use the following copyrighted material: excerpt from the poem, "*At Courmayeur*," from *Bernard Spencer, Complete Poetry, Translations & Selected Prose* (Bloodaxe Books, 2011).

For Sandy
(1956 -2010)
Darling, how did you think I could forget you,
you who forever stayed behind?
BERNARD SPENCER, *At Courmayeur*

TABLE OF CONTENTS

11

THE WOLF YEARLING

THE DESERT ELK

In time, this ceaseless wind will brush aside
the vulgar charm of exhausted huntsmen.
It sweeps dunes like breath on votive candles

to disinter a skeleton intact,
its limber touch laying bare the fragments,
leaving unharmed a larkspur's fringed petals.

Wind was body, seized in her own bloodbeat
or touched like birthwater warming her sides
for pleading mouths of calves. When it began

what she knew ranged far beyond petroglyphs
wrought in stone to mute gods, a shaman's scream.
When snowdrifts thawed into bright streams,

whose eyes could hers implore: I followed open
water, sagebrush, daylight fading cold and remote,
the bullet, by now, refusing return.

MY GREAT AUNT SPEAKS OF NIGHTS IN HARDIN COUNTY

Preachers said God made Texas nights this dark.
That's no comfort to girls home by themselves.
She could hear tongues and praises loud outside;
old wives, children, men of coal or lumber —
lots of folks shouting and carrying on,
given more to water-witching than prayer
come first light. It's how folks fought loneliness.

Beyond the plank steeples rising in swamps,
this fur trader's daughter spent nights alone,
her father trudging forgotten dirt trails
impassable to anything with wheels.
Bound for some reclusive trapper's cabin
he'd return by way of any roadhouse,
stumbling past the decay of tenant shacks.

She recalls those nights squinting through windows
waiting for his shadow to reemerge
soaked with rain and pelts — a feral hunter.
The last time I paid her a call, blindness
was slowly dimming her central vision.
Sometimes a stray voice makes her turn and look,
rain tapping glass like a startled stranger.

THE FATHER RETURNING

We bring him back to the place of his youth —
his Ithaca, hoping what fills his eyes
will be something from an earlier year
that soothes all perception back into place.

We reach the lakebed from a stretch of road
that threads the dry basin like a grey seam.
Our eyes hunt for storms tumbling above hills,
watch plovers flutter off alkali flats,

their brief flight regaining his native air.
The shorthand for it is *memory loss*,
the near-term fleeing as if never here
like the least tangible thing ever held.

But what came to him only made him wince,
the past's unyielding flume of images:
who lived down the street before troop trains came,
names of friends lost in Rommel's Africa.

We wanted him back, each thought honed and sheer,
nothing faltering on a puzzled tongue,
and his laughs piercing dusk like nightingales,
each spark unmediated by a mind's

relentless entangling of who and when,
to know us before his eyes lose our names
or the way a desert looks in the rain
after dust devils churn birds into air.

Ninemile Canyon, California

THE DESERT RANCHER ON SUNDAY

Winds release clouds from the tread of drifting
but buoy the arcs of loitering hawks.

It's so quiet he swears he hears sunlight,
Chihuahuan sage blossoming in clusters.

Where his footfalls impel a warbler's flight,
distant church bells summon their own echoes.

He kneels, presses palms to parched tractor ruts
that angle off into wind-runneled fields.

Thin soil keeps him for another season,
the ground made of nothing his hands won't hold.

MAPPING THE MIGRANT'S SHRINE
for Sonia Alvarado Soriano (1982-2007)

We swear they stand no chance facing this wind.
Who prospers here when heat conspires with stone
to gall votive candles down to slivers?

If Santa Barbara's a saint defrocked
there's patrons enough for any lost cause —
maybe St Jude will untangle roads north.

A new saint's image, pinned to granite, flies
above a young girl's photo. Loosed by wind,
she floats in the rain, the prowling future.

Arivaca, Arizona

LAST WORDS TO MY DAUGHTER TRANSPORTING A FOAL

for Amy, who went home tired

Horses learn evasion has its rewards.
But forget lead rope and halter for now.

Take the five-wheel trailer. That will work fine.
Drive slow — she'll brace when you accelerate.

Know they sweat from the need to stay balanced
through the anxiety of long travel.

Tinge her water with mint, or molasses.
The mare won't come, so nurse her with bottles.

Watch her bedding — sawdust irritates eyes.
Don't let vents blow air straight into her face.

I hope you planned your arrival early.
We've promised to train her. She's almost sure.

TIGER CREEK, SOUTH OF AGUILA, ARIZONA

It's early October. The twilight sun
releases the hours to a damp stillness
running lambent over the cooling ground.
My grandson, heedless of the failing light,
scoops small handfuls of sand over his legs,
his seven-year old mind playing wildly.

Out here, I think of Sundog, a rancher
who died four days shy of turning fifty.
While we'd sat and spoke on this very spot
he said he wanted a green burial —
just a pine box, and his Baptist preacher,
the drunk who kept the faith he never could.

As light's spent, and wind gathers speed and dust,
I coax my grandson out of his whimsy.
He laughs, runs homeward, leaving me behind,
like sand I'll end up washing from his shoes.

A Study in South Tucson

The parolee you met last night in town
is up this morning picking wildflowers.

His freedom's a slippery enterprise.
Trouble breaks rank and tracks him furtively.

At Café Catalonia, this new friend
says he can't touch his wife without a drink.

Jail is not the only type of hard time
he says, while wishing for vodka and ice.

As the bailiff's hands come cold to the touch,
blossoms break apart in the dry spring wind.

LATE SUMMER AT CAFÉ CATALONIA

I enter, and as the door slams behind
me, last night's wine bargains harsh with my skull.
With essential charm a waitress spies me:
"Good morning — anywhere you like," she says.
Truckers know that greeting like a safehouse.
With both her hands full of greasy dishes,
she carries a menu under her arm,
drops it on my table as she whisks by,
leaving a whiff of sweat, stale cigarettes
fused to cheap perfume, and disappointment.
She shouts hello to a man named Sundog.
Isn't this the place he'll always return,
his sad eyes saying he's permanent here?

This café is ruled by matrons like her —
all late middle-age, as if they'd been hired
from a class reunion, the year hushed up.
To a lone man who stands to leave, one says,
"No Beth today?" As she adjusts his warped
table, his reply is murmured bitter
while ranchers gab to her on what plagues them
in the field: worn gears, wind, terminal rust.
Her cook stays invisible. He's rumored
a fugitive paid under the table.
All that means is he's one of us at heart,
each life worn as fence posts, but welcomed here,
like letters we wrote but never sent home.

PASSAGE THROUGH THE CORDILLERA

Backpackers gather at the trailhead's gate.
They drag their shadows uphill behind them
where crescent wings of a white-throated swift
run some careless lizard to its dead end.

Weaving a nest of twigs and grass, its kin
built a home in a fortress of cholla.
Sunlight found the deep place in its hollow.
Then some human hand blocked it with a stone.

Out of my reach, I cannot remove it,
so I hike on in my trusty sneakers,
the soles well-worn to many a switchback,
slow to let go of the footprints beneath.

OVERTAKING THE UNION PACIFIC

I watch its churning engine spit heat
at the sun, exhaust a sheen nearly wet
against the foothills. Pecan groves

at Lobo fall behind us, leafless and alone.
Something draws the engineer and me
to want whatever's south, as cottonwoods

must want their green to rinse our eyes.
Horizons sleepwander here, like steam
from the 2 a.m. coffee cup of a woman

gone now into the past tense. After her,
all love is a raincheck. For now, we cut
this valley — broad as the Mare Imbrium,

the engineer behind his thick blue glass,
and all those towns, my unseen friend,
that were never ours. All those that were.

WHITE CANYON

False indigo thrives by roads where my jeep
lumbers south over a drought-seared mesa,
the world a sand trap for my orphaned tracks.
The fragrance of piñon suffuses winds
that lift the frail bodies of canyon wrens
and those trudging, black, iridescent crows
that glimmer through dust motes graining the light.

I descend petrified seas of rimrock
to the cooling shoreline of meltwater
that soothes the soles of my feet like cold flames.
My heels imprint the slickrock channel bed —
no mark that will last, unlike saurian
claw prints hardened beyond me downriver,
molded on Time's last super continent.

In Tanzania lie hominoid prints
held fast in the ash of three million years,
some so close abreast we might imagine
they were formed by pairs holding each other.
Perhaps one was a child held by the hand.
Or maybe two closed ranks just at the thought
one of their kin must reach down for a stone.

BLUES DESPITE THE ODDS

Silenced cotton gins and screened-in porches
line dusty arteries of hardpan roads
flayed into earth by frenzied hoof and tire.
Guitar riffs moan through the thick summer air
to breach the weather-beaten windowsills
of the unpainted frame house my aunt owned,
buzzing beveled glass and dark varnished wood.
She tells the photo of her dead husband
that fifes, fiddles, and drums are devil's play,
gospel sounds twisted by bands of foul tongues,
those penniless vagrants blighting our roads
to filch the ears of the weakest sinners,
leading good folk astray for a buck dance.
She died and never got the band names right —
how long could you screw up "Memphis Millie"?
We buried her with her husband's photo,
taking it off the mantelpiece. She swore
that man had the brightest eyes ever seen.

Vaqueros por La Vida

We swear they have no hope, these older ones
who won't quit, joints creaking like worn saddles
they ride, ardent in wind, boasting vain oaths
they'll forever beat death at its own game,
as they run but half the calves they used to
before drought withered grassland to parchment
under Arivaca's skies mute of storms.
Pickups have long replaced buckboard wagons
but branding irons still glow to propane
burning for calves subdued by rope, men's knees
on their throats to put beef on our tables.
At day's end these men will meander ground
with the sore stride of spent quarter horses,
always going someplace they fail to reach,
inversions for what can't be gained elsewhere
when no one bets they come back for the rain.

North of San Lázaro

Mesquite fences stretch like saurian spines
across fields overrun by buffel grass.
The government told him to string steel chains
between bulldozers and drag it all clean.
Cows shift between paddocks like dull legions
daydreaming the cool shade of mesquite bosques
as jaguars clamber north from Mexico.
Where storms clear in premonitions of light
old disputes slacken their grip on his mind,
releasing his hours for walks down old trails
in fluttering shadows of cottonwood.
There the coatis forage manzanita
in places once spread with picnic baskets.
He stoops to mend the loose gabion stones
that slow and widen his thinning river,
walls that kindle a progeny of reeds.
He feels the easy slide of silt through hands
inscribed with scars from years in gravel mines
that paved highways for other men's journeys.
The water sounds like women whispering.
Something in the voices will clear his name.

WINTER FOOTHILLS
for Tobi

We climbed out of Sierras, bending down
on a steep switchback to look for fossils.
Then in the twilight of vanishing day
she gathered close in a downcanyon wind,
the sun like brass in the cottonwood limbs.
Our shadows trailed us through the arroyo,
their molten forms warping on the cutbank.

Above us, summits whispered of blizzards.
That day's hunt only yielded trace fossils —
those death marks of vacant anatomies,
though I'd promised a trove of trilobites.
But her blue eyes have long endured my schemes,
transfixed in my evenings of soft words,
the way storms come when ice might split the trees.

THE COTTON WEST OF HOCKLEY COUNTY

Some say it's grace to inherit this land,
fields having all the labored memory
they could hold. When the droughts came, my uncle
choked back blasphemy rising in his throat.

His life wore out for three bales per acre.
Fickle storms often failed to soak to depth
and minds schemed hard to find hope of harvest.
He'd lay phosphorous and deep-break the soil,

spray for aphids just to see new blights come.
Fretting the longevity of worm gears
in the pivots of irrigation arms,
technology fees finally drained him.

Not far off, hawks coast on thermal circuits,
their cries pulling day back into being.
They touch the earth through the sweltering air,
the deed to the land now fresh in my fist.

TRAIN STATION, BENSON, ARIZONA. YEAR UNKNOWN

Behind a smoky and faded window
the stationmaster endures like envy,
surveys rail cars against summer's night sky.
Air's so candent even a kiss could warp.

In that apparitional semi-dark,
he sees a woman straining with luggage —
a traveler's ritual of burden.
Despite the conductor's merciless clock
he makes time to heft her bags to porters.

This woman, whose age you can't quite resolve,
becomes the last person to board your coach.
Unsure if she embarked alone, you watch
as a stranger helps her remove her coat.
Settling in an aisle seat, she smiles her thanks.

Now you see appear what must be her son.
To the stranger, who resumed his silence,
she claims boys easier to raise than girls,
as the boy rifles through a homemade lunch
in what strikes you as unnamed urgency.

Trundling north, the train pauses at stations
where no one gets off, none on the platforms
to even deny that your train is theirs,
no stop empty enough to need your name.

HOW WE SPOKE BEYOND HANAUPAH CREEK, DEATH VALLEY

Snowfall lay soft as an opium dream
over the Panamint Range. Untold
elevations below, in the fine-grained
heat of late fall, we mounted boulders
studded with feldspar. What wind carried
and lost melded amid salmon-orange
wings of butterflies edging our silence.

I cut for you a sprig of desert holly, illicit
but vindicated because I said it would grow
back, unlike the bladed crystals you stole
from that small quarry near Warm Springs.

We seized the bright rush of that day, its sky
clear as the eye of God. With a tenuous faith
in our shaky Jeep — parked facing downhill,
we returned west to our seaboard city
lined with lofty sweetgums and maples,
each avenue a slow burial in leaves.

NIGHTFALL ON THE BAJADA

Ocotillo blossoms when it pleases.
The yucca will only blossom in dark,
their flowers clustered like monks at vespers.
Rain may dry before it reaches the ground
where boquilla streams still flow into creeks.

Beyond the quickened nerves of Inca doves
that huddle as thickly as mesquite bosques,
coyotes ambush a black-tailed jack
to feed pups in deserted badger dens.
Men breach canyons that throw back their voices.

MY SISTER WAITS WITH MAMAGRANDE OUTSIDE SANTA TERESITA'S

Her new white organdy communion dress
can't keep insect bites from the blood that's theirs.
Still, Mamagrande grips her rosary.

Dust settles across verbena and skin.
It's so hot they feel heat rising from stones.
Sweat scuttles down each spine like God's finger.

Along this Sunday plaza promenade
boys and girls swelter through the state of grace.
The ageless sun surges into their lines.

From birth she was raised by Mamagrande,
who grew calla blooms for her hair; and I,
a red carnation for her folded hands.

Near Cananea

Penitents' prayers plead effigies of saints,
the wooden forms brought like wounded soldiers
down twilight streets of Sonoran cities
where norteño ballads flood the night air.

Resurrected by late summer monsoons,
modest rivers undulate through valleys.
They pass reed corrals of poor ranchitos
and arc wide through the distant bajadas
of mesquite trees and creosote bushes.

One farmer grips a shallow-bladed plow
pulled by unequalled yoke of horse and mule.
His cattle and goats drift through grassy fields,
their living hides unconcerned with buzzards
weaving their circuit above a dead colt.

Concrete archangels guard the camposanto
where cotton candy and balloons are sold
by peddlers on The Day of the Dead.
Widows plant maravilla for loved ones.
They say San Isidro makes fresh rains come,
drenching strangers till they're part of the storm.

TERLINGUA

For the opulent lust of cinnabar, men
could once die here in three languages.

Man and stone need every hour
of darkness to exhale the sun's fire.

Adobe's faithful to legend — roofs are gone,
spelled by the sky's enameled blue skull.

I step through a gate and on down a slope
that fans into the dull green of creosote

to find a Model T, skeletal in oxidized
decay, crows cawing its indigent anthem.

Lightning spikes the Chisos Mountains,
like strands of a woman's hair, disquieted

into silver, where she stands in afterlight,
the dust unswept from her doorway.

COWBOYS

With his package of refused letters
returned unread to him at Long Binh Jail,
he came back early from Vietnam
to the ranch he would inherit in west
Oldham County. There, he considers
the panorama unfolding around him
of worn fence posts canting in the wind
like drunks against a balustrade, the wire
guarding the cattle his son calls by name.

LAST WORDS TO AN OLD MINER LEAVING ALBUQUERQUE

Jacob, this day storms whip those same tree limbs
your feet stumbled home under. And dizzy
with winds, you'd argue the compass, pounding

strangers' doors to query them with maps. Once,
your paychecks came tough as Roman galleys
when sleep filled your nights with groaning timbers.

Forlorn as those mining towns were, and cold,
if clean winds now mean your lungs wake easy,
you can't curse streets here like dreams chipped away

each time mines closed, depleted by the war.
Why say nothing's here for you? Why blame storms
and wars, or maps at the mercy of rain?

ONE SON SOUTH TO RIO BRAVO

Few can ditch the trap of mining town jobs —
a rock rolled uphill forever from hell.
My brother from Nueva Rosita
chased silver in the Sierra Madre,
insatiable as a flock of grackles.
But reality was high desert coal
turning lungs black as onyx rosaries
in the frail fists of village faith healers.

I tried to tell him the good life's a ranch,
heaven on earth this dusty sierra.
Where nights once feared the arson of Cortés
a world rose on leather, rope, wire, and hope,
hard work in alfalfa bales and fence posts.
When hot whirlwinds thrash man and beast with dust,
prayers plead skies will bless us with rain. If not,
we'll earn the wingspan of buzzards for shade.

OVERHEARD BETWEEN WACO AND JUBILEE SPRINGS

I don't get it. You want me to believe
God took Adam out of ground he called *good* —
the soil that nurtured the downfall of Man
when the lurid skin of one small apple
was polished by heat of one woman's tongue.
The road out of Eden became one-way.

You say that's the reason the last preacher
I confessed my liquor-and-whore sins to
ran off with my wife and stole the stained glass
out of the most broke-down church poor folk built
in McLennan County. He left us cold.
Left his sermons still burning in my fields.

THE EVANGELIST AT THE BRAZOS RIVER

Crowds converge six miles west of Knox City
where diggers once chased clues of mammoth bones.
A man's voice cuts through air like Pharaoh's whips.
If crowds believe salvation is shouted —

peril's alarm at the edge of mercy,
then today the lost become disciples,
get baptized in the silt-laden Brazos.
On this same ground where backsliders slink off,

old time believers plead hard to sinners,
wave bibles as if all are near-sighted,
holding the Word up in the humid whirl
of people wilting in a July sun

that flogs each one as if they're flagellants
in rituals of distant continents.
Rising, the saved go their ways, sins forsworn,
the Lord's songs flowing from hymn-famished lips.

Like hard weather that blows in from nowhere
the evangelist will return next year,
just to win us back, again and again.
Sinners reborn without a memory.

OPEN RANGE

Daylight comes warm against the rust
of a thresher. Runoff from storms
lies shadowed in the mesquite grove.
Night's coyotes scatter like spies,
slinking off to recondite shade.

The day's too dust-laden for speech.
Wind sings through what falls out of use,
a refrain of discordant notes
threading rusted pump rods, fencing,
a screen door beyond the back porch.

THE FARMER'S DAUGHTER IN LATE SUMMER

This heavy soil is never kind to peanuts,
a hard earth that won't forget boundaries.
Subsoil moisture runs marginal at best.

With day burning down to lazy shadows,
ozone enriches the air like hoofbeats
to bait the yield of any crop to come.

She watches her dad scan emergent plants
and wipe his brow in beleaguering heat,
as if sweaty sleeves gave any relief.

Here, life is irrigation and timing,
machinery still gauged by rules-of-thumb;
riddles men like him hold in the balance.

Peanuts and cotton must be harvested
together — like her twin sisters at birth.
"Love this ground, it loves ya back," her dad claims.

Hearing those pensive sighs, she leaves him be.
He'll ponder yields like a wild game warden
surmising the path of the next stampede.

Closing the door of her new pickup truck,
she waves goodbye to that smiling man, squints
in the rearview mirror to read his lips.

LETTER FROM YUMA TO MY FATHER BACK EAST

You think my skies are so blue they're boring.
That I've gotten this desert air all wrong,
and don't need the jaded heat of sand dunes,
nor horizons widened to jagged peaks
of mountains named for saints homesick for Spain,
pointing stone fingers at constellations
rolling through a night's un-blighted circuits.

It is you who needs his afternoon skies
harried to storms so gray you turn English
with rain, and rain was the war you hated
when your bomber limped home on one engine.
What did you feel when pilots feathered the props,
your navigator an ape with sextant,
plexiglas blinded by fog hard as salt?

New Jersey's the center of the cosmos —
or so you say, the place your sons can thrive,
though my last joke about it turned you dour.
But you're just wistful over tiresome holes
you made me dig to plant fruit trees long dead
when fading hurricanes whipped Sea Bright raw,
and you knew I'd quit school soon and leave home.

Today, winds arise like lost travelers.
Dawn came deranged by threats of rare weather.
I'll get this letter out soon as I can.
Don't fear too much blue for me. Soon enough,
monsoons will shake this desert clean with floods,
thunder will thread night skies shut with nimbus.
Wild rain will loose me from a dream of home.

FORECLOSURE IN LATE AUTUMN

His family's last night in the farmhouse
passed in silence. None dreamed of wrecking crews.
After sleet and wind spellbound the sleepers
they woke to a world of windfall apples.

Near concrete silos as dead as dolmans,
dark fills the ruts of his last thresher run.
Two forage harvesters, the grain augur,
and stalls, await the clutch of public sale.

For auctioneers, no weather is too grim;
bidders line up in good time, and shudder.
What's in "fair condition" means fair plunder
for the crowds served lunch in local church halls.

Irrigation wells had just been repaired.
They lure crows like hordes of drunken tourists,
their shrieks filling skies with barren echoes.
Feds could sell it all cheap as Roman slaves.

These mist-shrouded fields were a universe.
Harvests dozed against good autumn bounties
hour by hour, before years of flagging yields,
new sleet unfurling, again and again.

NINEVEH, TEXAS

Sometimes we really are where the worst
rumors place us. This town's no one's useful
getaway. Our naming was prophecy

for a future in sackcloth. Enough fences lost
last year to wildfires put all in penitent garb.
Drought means no one skips a chance to repent.

Residents have thinned so much over years,
those of us left need our own shady leaves
to shelter the scorch of derelict love.

If they tally hunting in the county statistics
then we're as Nineveh of old, our rowdies
like bas-relief lions come alive after dark.

Call me one more man who dreams escape —
Galveston Bay forever, landlocked no longer,
a good charter's wake to disquiet the shore.

THE THIRD MESA

The ancient settlements have weathered-down
to slim verdant windrows of remnant springs
that skein the outlines of vanished sheep pens
like sunk amphorae tracing crumbling ships.
Winged seeds of saltbush filter past snakeweed
in the light of a sun arcing through buttes
to tune ceremonies lapsed to silence.
The past remains in pigmented handprints
pressed to the weaving of log-and-brush roofs;
timeless, frantic, after the peace was signed.

BONNIE CLAIRE FLAT, DEATH VALLEY

Fossils stake claims in countries of mute bone,
dolomite and limestone mined for cement
that burns beneath me in the LA heat
where I left worries too deep to answer.
I climb again to where this desert waits.
Seas were here before mountains rose to ice —
those tall undertakers of extinction
for untold generations of shellfish
abandoned to desiccating lakebeds
to vanish like Old Testament armies.

Beyond me, in the Calico Mountains,
fragments of camels and three-toed horses
lie in dispersed and exotic arrays
like the plunder of Roman carnivals.
My driftwood campfire ignites easily
as I watch the frozen meteorites
flare in short-lived signatures above me,
the temperate pulse of night wind rising
along the trails darkening to the east.
The desert rustles like unnamed secrets.

THE SEASONAL WORKER

Harvest season wakens in Dome Valley.
He lives in his pickup he parks off-road,
sleeps there like Caliban under his cloak.
At dawn, sore muscles summon his body
to roll out of the truck and into fields.
Nearly alone, he's a figure stranded,
sudden successor to border crackdowns
that thinned laborers down to a trickle,
their absence like a poorly timed punch line.
College kids come, but bolt after a day,
fair weather moon-calves as ever there were,
thinking winter lettuce earns easy cash.
Cars pass like spies on the periphery.
The drivers stare down our long empty rows,
point to the few backs bending in the sun,
speed off to LA, certain they survive.

LATE LIGHT IN THE SANTA CRUZ VALLEY

If you can dismiss the moon's pale ascent
you might hear wingbeats in the fading light,
dusk calling hawks to perch in cottonwoods
and toll a deadpan vigilance eastward
toward sierras that ruddle to shadows.

These hawks are connoisseurs of what it takes
to die when small prey barters noonday sun
for nightfall's cooling of dry riverbeds,
waiting out the heat under my trailer.
Canted on one wheel, it tilts back to earth.

Storm Light

Beyond our metal-pipe corral
that stands calm through rust and survives,
I mend dirt roads rutted by squalls.

My grandson, roused from a late nap,
can't wait to drench his new sneakers
in fresh puddles his feet have found,

his mother infuriated
at this boy's primal rite of mud.
The thin limbs of a lightning-scorched

tree, tilted like a drunk giant,
lures his four-year old hands to flex
and touch leaves suddenly in reach.

I stood by the catchment, watching,
weighing any hint of danger —
shard or branch, or uncoiling eyes,

thinking of a way to explain
why I brand yearlings for shipment.
That's when he grabbed the warbler's nest,

eyes tracing flights of startled birds,
as if his lungs could breathe their songs
into that pale opening sky.

DEAD RECKONING IN THE PUERTO BLANCO MOUNTAINS

Storm winds cool asphalt where the highway ends.
Rich creosote owns the air in my lungs.
I always drift where topo maps go wrong
and locals warn: return the way you came.
Rock cairns are the oldest profession here.
It's dusk now, so I'm done stumbling on scree
as sharp as the spurs of conquistadors,
and pitch my tent where bursage is windbreak.

Piling scraps of kindling I'd held all day,
I hear the rustle of other hikers.
A young woman approaches my campfire,
asks about GPS coordinates.
Ashamed, I mumble that I'm obsolete,
show her my compass and my haggard map.
Thin desert leaves turn face-up. No rains come,
only that burnt mesquite smell of her hair.

THE STABLEMAN
for James Welch

That Sunday you groomed the palomino
a mountain lion leapt down on her back,
laying bare that sudden bloody ribcage
old veterinarians would stitch up
after she bolted to slam the big cat
against the limb of a storm-split mesquite.
On some nights you might recall bustling youths
that rode her down summer trails in years past
even as she grew weaker in the hips,
that aged gait over polished creek stones.
On some nights you might taste the buoyant dust.

COPPER CUT ROAD, SANTA RITA RANGE

Late shadows glide over the desertscape.
They scuttle over sun-ripened larkspur,
drift through cutbanks and the lithic scatter
of vanquished tribes. Some shadows once ferried
their survival across the last Ice Age.
Other shadows have long since left the earth,
as if they had resigned their tenure here,
coming to lie still in canyons or caves
where they overlapped, waiting for thunder.

DESERT LITTORAL

Winter swells this occasional river —
runoff from mountains in the Tucson sun.
Time-whitened boulders jut like broken teeth.

My six-year old, with his Tonka dump truck,
really thinks the world's never heard his schemes.
With a stick he probes alluvial sand.

His treasure's flat stones he says I can skip,
so I sidearm them on the current's face.
But twigs we just toss in, toy ships at sea.

THE WOLF YEARLING

The elk that eluded her as a pup
has been rotting in a trap for a year.

The lair she was born one April nightfall
was home to coyotes shot last summer.

She'll waver at the numberless campfires
before yielding to human redolence,

fur bristling in wind that carries their scents
as if to teach her how the dead survive.

COYOTE IN A VOLCANIC FIELD

Through the dead hollow of the cinder cone
she threads past lava spires, as sand-charged wind
tries to flay us all down to arid dust.
Looping and backtracking on trails I walked
in a half-futile hunt for garnet gems,
she digs for small prey — comes up with nothing,
but quenches her thirst on indigent streams.
Heir to the throne of vanished sabertooths,
hers is a raw and casual reign now,
dark movement breaking a highway's mirage.

FIRST SNOW IN THE SANTA CATALINAS

Mountain snowmelt from winter's early storms
renews the laggard pace of flagging streams.
Waves, sediment-rich, furrow the desert,
forking westward like untangling voices
tamping ground with a dark, insistent breath.

Curious teens wade into soft shallows.
On the other shore, a man shows his sons
something flowing past the soft embankment
in front of their feet. They stare, visitors
watching a small and unrehearsed death.

WIDOWER AT THE HASSAYAMPA RIVER

In the quiet steps of his daydreaming, hawks
unclasp trees and scissor the fading light
into segments of distance, as he fits life
to the dark shape of cool wind following him.
Over a riverbottom path feeding winter
cottonwoods that thread their roots through
ancestral bones, the smoldering campfires,
like votive candles lit by staid supplicants,
are already less than once upon a time.

OUR SKETCH OF DEATH VALLEY

Throughout the day, we mounted switchbacks
white with salt, thorn-guarded climbs that met
strengthening heat and droughted air, our eyes
squinting past the burnt silence of distance.

We'd camped along the base of a wide net
of gravel that swept downhill from a nameless
canyon, mesquite shading us all night
from nothing but the stars.

This is where the earth widens and tilts
at less than glacial strides, as if being pried
apart by some indolent Poseidon, men
and myth tasting the silence of extinction.

Whatever's beneath us lays embalmed
in strata, burned to worn traces of borax
trenches astride milling works left
to the weather-beaten typeface of desert,
pulleys and flywheels frozen corsets of rust.

At dusk, we left the falling sun to trawl
a final swath over the salt pan of dead ocean,
dried-up over millennia, dust leaching
into the afterwarmth of hours as it floated
back to us from the soundless places.

A RAVEN RETURNS TO THE SALTON SEA

Your flight runs the girth of human fables
scrawled dark on some Medieval palette.
One tale even swears when God fixed the sun
to burn in the incompressible night,
the ravens saw Icarus in His thoughts.

Now you skim this raw and unfabled wind.
Welcome back. You may resume surveillance
over hawks you hope leave you the road kills.
Maybe you'll relieve a wren of its wings,
its bantam shadow now clutching the earth.

Travertine Point, Santa Rosa Mountains

MARQUISE DRIVE IN WINTER

Late walks spare you a long day's tedium.
You circle the neighborhood at sundown,
pass an empty house up for sale by folks
you've never met in the years you've lived here;
its courtyard, inner rooms, no more dim now
for the lights or loves that vacated them.

The half-moon runs mirrored in high windows.
Mesquite smoke that sweetens the late year's dusk
drifts up from chimineas beyond sight.
It melds with the flights of emerging bats —
those airborne voyeurs skirting the distance,
curving hard angles in the cooling wind.

LATE WINTER BIRDING IN DEVIL'S PUNCHBOWL
for Doug Peacock

His shadow follows him over sandstone
that warps up between fault lines named for saints.
For him, stumbling out of breath down pinyon
trails always made sense after Vietnam.

Coming to track finches and fox sparrows
before their winter wings flee for summer,
he'll fend the cold with a flask of false fire,
arrive at the place none of them appear.

LEAVING CIPRIANO PASS

Spanish priests burned brittlebush for incense
but Satan owned this ground when prospectors
bleached to stone on its broiling routes to gold.
Seems they had no "interpretive trail" out.
You could say thirst is handmaiden to hell.
Creosote burgeons up through their graves now
as if to warn men they too know shortcuts.
Warblers and wild sheep share each other's dust
in beleaguered damps of hollow bedrock
that clutches water like petrified wombs.
They say they were sacred to vanished tribes.
Though my mouth's as dry as cinder cones here,
I don't think I'd boil clean that seething swill —
I'd rather keep my impenitent thirst.
Near dusk, hikers trace lines on tourist maps
of some cartographer's jagged path out.
Their eyes connect the map's route with real ground
as if they were pleading with a closed door.
That route we'll follow till it disappears.

Tinajas Atlas Mountains, Arizona

AMARGOSA RIVER
for Larry D. Thomas

My jeep's in arrowweed a long mile back.
I forsake calendars, begin again,
sky falling over the horizon's rim.

The sage sparrow at the margin of sight
builds a sparse twig nest hidden under shrubs.
Smoke from a driftwood campfire burns my eyes.

In the millstone of wind, millennia,
dead railspurs cool under cloud penumbras.
Storms will arrive to swell the gaunt river,

water infusing shriveled clay and silt,
deferring its boneshape of extinction.
Plovers, hawks, will chase its reborn surface —

blue flicker of pupfish and speckled dace,
sharpened inquiry by dark wing and eye,
cool ripples just beginning to shimmer.

THE YOUNG VISITOR IN SENITA BASIN

With eyes the soft blue of palo verde,
she's dwarfed by rhyolite and breccia —
those igneous giants of petrified time.
The wilderness is open as her palm
that will find the dull red flame of jasper.

She listens to wind and begins to hear
the green voices of juniper, piñon;
pictures sidewinders in canyon wren nests
but won't witness those same nests washed away
down storm-filled arroyos come late summer.

At school, she'll sketch a sloth or mammoth,
give her report to teacher and classmates
on the park ranger's tales of vanished seas,
the white flare of night-blooming cereus,
and each stone hearth still arcing toward the light.

LAST LIGHT AT STRONGHOLD CANYON

Gaunt mesquite threw a pretence of shadow,
doing what it could to cool my trespass.
I crossed the creek bed stained brown by tannins
from the mountain snowmelt, watched the pupfish
and minnows swim a tide pool's gathered depth.

When I knelt to cup water to my lips
I saw where a cougar had gone ahead
of me, angling-off into peaks above,
trampling a switchback born of its hunger.

Looking upward, I watched a hawk orbit,
man and beast in the clear flame of her eyes
that fielded us under the rising moon
as we turned back for what passes for home,
shadows falling into an open field.

CLIMBING CAP ROCK TRAIL WITH MY DAUGHTER

Watch how the snow falls lambently tonight
from these same blue altitudes the sun scorched
us, in months that own the graves of water.
Below, near the first pullout at the two-
or three-thousand-foot level, we had scanned
the valley floor, the two of us who begged
for winter, backlit now by this first snow
pulling its white robe over stone and fir,
hawks afloat in icy currents of air,
each sinuous god in wind-stiffened flight
above thorns of mesquite, spines of cholla,
a runnel's icy churn and slant of fall —
tributary to canyons far below,
and us at 9,000 feet, breath turned steam
as dusk persuades us to windbreaks of pine
where I find your eyes blinking back the snow.

LAND SURVEY IN THE AMARGOSA VALLEY

Where by all accounts I should have been
back in my LA office, I'm out here on roads
inscribed on maps in broken hashmarks,
like dashes in a fading book of Morse
Code, graded dirt and a high clearance
all someone figures desert workers need
to trundle through bursage and creosote.

Now the dusk shades to darkness
in the depth of cutbanks that wall
riparian willows along a thin river
cleaving the alluvium and hardpan
of the valley floor. The western sky
fades to the color of exotic moths.
In the deepening horizon, lightning
throws ghost-light over vast fields
of cinder and ash spewed by volcanoes,
inert now in the shape of prehistory.

All day, figures danced through the heat
shimmering any surface laid with asphalt —
illusions deserts play with in distances,
like hippie-chick hitchhikers we gave up
trying to find, decades ago, to hold
whatever heat their bodies could give us,
in the rooms they would almost sleep in.

THEY NEVER LEAVE WACO, EVEN WHEN YOU JUMP
THEIR CARS

No, Patsy with her fallen angel's-eye view
of the world insisted she give me a ride
in her '74 Duster — its benediction of Pall Mall
after-breath — to my job on the Union Pacific,
her awe of radio everything I hate, all them
4-digit AM spots in love with church oldies
and livestock shows and God knows what
when all I wanted was to walk the Brazos alone
that morning, even with rain and wind coming on
and pushing my collar up like a nightstick, the stench
of feedlots and diesel that coffee won't ever rinse
from lungs or bones, and where the usual hag
hawks boiled peanuts like hymnals to choirs,
forgetting I said *no* at least twenty times — the same
number of years I've wanted to go east forever,
quitting polite obligations to Patsy's AM dials
and whatever here needs this chokehold town,
to say nothing of its rain, dank enough at midnight
to make me reach for a voice that isn't there.

How We Woke One Year in Lobo, Texas

The welcome sign mocked a Cold War Vegas.
So much sky's out there you'd think its blue weight
would buckle the very ground we stood on.
When we sank in the hotel's warped mattress
we didn't impress the Vacancy sign.
Squinting through our first-floor window, I saw
dust devils cakewalk a drought-crippled pool.

Pulling herself from sleep, Janice asked me
not to snuff my damned Winstons in her beer
because she wasn't quite done with it yet,
as she fidgeted — the new ghost-habit
of fetching her own smokes she'd tried to quit
last week. When she rose, the sun-flashed torrent
of red hair down the ripple of her spine

said she could be one of Hopper's women,
lit that fleeting way loneliness can make
a woman more beautiful than she is,
why I never failed to say loving her
is easy as jaywalking a ghost town.
Off to bathe, she'd paused at the radio
to pull Joan Baez down from faint airwaves,

asked if I'd recalled the song. I said yes,
but there's no tea or oranges from China
in hotels named Thunderbird, west of God.
That's when I saw in the mirror that wry
smile carving an odd angle on her face.
I've heard that men elsewhere have clearer signs
than smiles to read. Still others, none at all.

Why You Can Never Cure a Small-town Heart

Because the town is fried food, if nothing else,
thick odors of cooking grease warping blacktop.

On account of patrons, stared-down by neon
or hope, never break faith with a future not theirs.

For the very fact that rows of empty bleachers hold
a silence all their own, silhouetting a lost season.

Because a lone dancer in the only bar lifts the rich coal
of her hair to fan the sweat tickling her spine.

For the reason that when a band ignites a dance floor
much depends on which way a woman's shadow leans.

Because weekends are clean echoes of the last one,
and engines are gunned to beat the red lights home.

TRAVELOGUE FOR A NEVADA JANUARY

It has taken me restive hours to drag myself
from bed at the Atomic Inn, my fingers
too cold to practice the cornet I'm due to play
at a gig tonight in Vegas, fired from the last
one when my solo went flat. Losing the battle
to chase last night's booze from my skull, I light
a Turkish cig I'd bummed from a somewhat lady
hitchhiking outside a brothel, and follow white

neon to Rebel Mart. No one here this crazy early
but truckers and drifters. One trucker strains
not to scream at an aged clerk who can't find
a pack of Camel 99s right in front of his dull
face. Watching the clerk falter is like watching
an ancient film clip skipping frames. Out the door,
I wrap my fist around my coffee, bend into wind
that funnels its bitter howl down Watson Street,

freezing me through holes in shoes the last
good woman warned me to chuck weeks ago
when they'd lost all identity as footwear. By late
afternoon, that Rebel Mart trucker watches Camel
smoke un-billow into cottonwood limbs at a Utah
truck stop. The clerk back in Beatty is finally
off shift, his wife clocking in, and I'm long
on Rt. 160 east as it rises and falls towards Vegas.

Beyond us all, the Panamint Mountains reach
high and cold enough to keep snowfall thick.
A young girl is on an outing with her weekend
dad. With a new storm building, he's uneasy
about the road back down the valley. He starts
the car, lets the warmth begin to surge about
his feet as his daughter, still outside, laughs
and grins. She leaves her angel in the snow.

No Texas Beyond Our Memory

When our grandfathers swore they loved the way
this dirt smelled, thunderheads never seemed far off.
But our fields are so dim now, you'd think herds

were eating ashes where prayers commit hard to rain
our five-year-old son's never seen. Sand storms
are so resolute they'd field-strip a rabbit's ass.

This drought gropes furrowed ground wheat and cotton
lost faith in, our world gone to moonscape, the raw
void of lunar dust that contour-plowing can't heal.

As cotton loads scale back, Annie's gin yard runs
rich with silence. Little can flourish, save mesquite,
roots tapping groundwater — never out of reach,

verdant canopies staring back at our poverty.
What water remains mocks our days when ropes
and chains must rescue cows mired in pond dregs.

At night, dust fine as talc laagers-up in corners.
Diminished wind sweeps it under the doorways
of our neighbors turning deadbolts in the dark.

DIVERTING SOUTH FROM BUCKHORN TANK

Daybreak spills into undulant shadows
scrabbling down Agua Caliente Hill.

The moon drifts to some other continent,
bearing off the one song a night bird knows.

This less-traveled country becomes mercy
belying alarms of unfinished maps.

Trails written by storms always feel like home,
last night's campfire still warm as forgiveness.

By the loose granite rolling underfoot
lie tracks I won't think more careless than mine.

Past the dusty gleam of human hunger
a puma drinks from the water's darkness.

RENAMING THE EARTH

We perch the four-wheeler on a slight rise,
lodge it firm behind an unyielding stump
of tired mesquite where late August monsoons
swell the Gila River west of Phoenix.
Its stones will burn all year for these few days
of immersion in a flow releasing
chubs and pupfish to glisten their ruddled-
silver skin, as if this flood's forever.
Crumbling its cutbanks, the river will push
jagged torrents of spent storms far beyond
our sight, as if to shout itself alive.
As we crawl the shallow current we feel
the season's heat drain from our summer blood.
Stripped down to bare flesh, sky throws a shadow
cast by hawks across the rise of your breasts.
As I rest my head in your lap, I reach
to shield your blue eyes from a sun that finds
the red waves of your hair singing with light.

HOMEWARD FROM AUSTIN

The road becomes a single lane into the absence
of all you knew. Foreclosed houses dimmed
heavy with despair line the street of your return,
holes in the memory of no one you know now.
Certainly not the young girl selling lemonade
to no visible customer. Not the homeless pair,
their tinder-parched forms recumbent under broken
lattice of some abandoned porch. Nor the old
woman mowing her lawn, a crone neighborhoods
like these never lose, where high noon finds
the young girl impatient to sell in Dixie cups
a lemonade that weakens from melting ice.
Watching her lips move soundlessly, you know girls
from this town never go far — few with fresh starts,
most taking anchorage in this deadbeat county —
an embedded chamber play. But you shift into drive
and leave, good in the hope that she'll make
it out a decade from now — if she's ever lucky,
worn down but content, and not ever going home.

DESERT MOUNTAIN SUNDAY
for Billy Higgins, who'd rather fly there with a jetpack

Through cauterized hollows of campsite
Fire pits, the raspy breath of an alpine
breeze is surmounted by hawks that rally
their wings in primal echelons. They marshal
beneath cumulus buildups in white mimic
of barges — clouds that'll soon shade field mice
who learn late that nothing riding updrafts starves.
In the Santa Cruz Valley below, a grandson
and grandfather put the hours in abeyance
for a gas grill and cooler. The boy watches
the man wipe smoky sweat from his eyes
with the back of a hand that grips a greasy
spatula. Shielding his own eyes, the boy gazes
up the Santa Catalina peaks, traces hawks arcing
down the long cool distance of the storm
where high winds thread pitch-dark feathers.
Rain begins to touch his face, and he pulls
his grandfather's free arm round his shoulder
as poplar leaves gust between their footsteps.

ABOUT THE AUTHOR

Jeffrey C. Alfier is a three-time Pushcart Prize nominee, and a 2010 nominee for the UK's Forward Prize for Poetry. In 2012, he was nominated for a Breadloaf scholarship. In 2006, he received honorable mention for the Rachel Sherwood Poetry Prize, and in 2005 won first place awards from the Redrock Writer's Guild of Utah and the Arizona State Poetry Society. He holds an MA in Humanities from California State University at Dominguez Hills. Having served twenty-seven years in the U.S. Air Force, he is a member of Iraq and Afghanistan Veterans of America (IAVA). He's also worked as a functional analyst with Science Applications International Corporation, and once taught history for City College of Chicago's European Division. In addition to journals cited herein, his credits include *Birmingham Poetry Review, Connecticut Review, Tulane Review, Pea River Journal, Los Angeles Review, New York Quarterly, Pearl Magazine* and *Poetry Ireland Review*. His chapbooks are *Strangers Within the Gate* (2005), *Offloading the Wounded* (2009), *Before the Troubadour Exits* (2010), *Bluesman's Daughter* (2010), *The Torch Singer* (2011), *The Gathering Light at San Cataldo* (2012), and *The City Without Her* (2012). He serves as co-editor of *San Pedro River Review*.